WITHDRAWN

D0598909

NOW MAKE THIS

CURATED BY
THOMAS BÄRNTHALER

Φ

CONTENTS

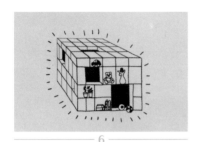

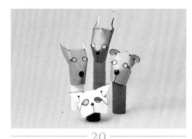

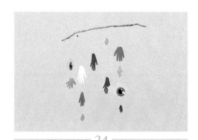

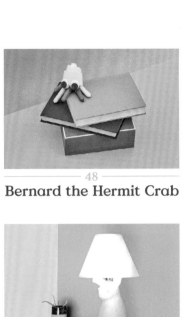

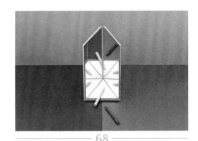

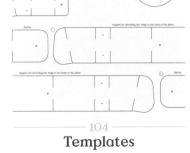

INTRODUCTION

Your chair, your lamp, the room you're in, your bed, your schoolbag, your shoes, and even your underwear — all of these things were thoughtfully created by designers. It is their job to imagine new things, and work out exactly how to make them. Most designers loved making things when they were children. Whether they built cities from sticks, or spaceships out of plastic bottles, they were able to turn their childhood passions into their careers. For most of them, buying a product is all well and good, but making a product is much more rewarding. Whatever you make by yourself is one of a kind, and just exactly the way you want it to be. Most of all, making things (for yourself or a friend) is so much fun!

You will find 24 projects in this book to make from scratch, including simple furniture for your room, cool toys, shoes, instruments, and even your own playhouse. Each project has been specially created by a world-class designer, which means you won't find these in any store! Each project tells you exactly what tools and materials you will need, roughly how much it will cost, and how much time it will take to make. Some of the projects require adult help, so make sure you have a fun-loving grown-up handy!

As you start working, you'll see that these projects can be adapted and personalized. Feel free to experiment a bit by changing them, or even trying something completely unique. And don't worry if it doesn't turn out quite the way you expected it to. Sometimes what you might think is a mistake can actually make your project even better!

Most designers still make time to play and experiment — that's how the best ideas are discovered. Who knows, maybe you'll grow up to be a designer one day! This is a very good place to start.

— Thomas Bärnthaler

PROJECT KEY:

!	◉ 0 TO $15 ◉ ◉ $15 TO $25 ◉ ◉ ◉ $25+	⧗ 15 TO 30 MINUTES ⧗ ⧗ 30 TO 60 MINUTES ⧗ ⧗ ⧗ 60 MINUTES +
INDICATES THAT THE PROJECT REQUIRES HELP FROM AN ADULT	**INDICATES HOW MUCH THE PROJECT WILL COST**	**INDICATES HOW LONG THE PROJECT WILL TAKE**

NOTE REGARDING MATERIALS:

Before you get started on a project, you will need to gather all the necessary materials and tools. Follow the materials list to find and collect what you need. Some of the materials and tools in this book will need to be bought, but you will probably have most everyday things — like pencils, pens, rulers, scissors, glue, staplers, tape, rubber bands, safety pins, and string at home already. There are also lots of materials you can fish out of the recycling bin, like newspaper, pieces of cardboard, plastic bottles, unwanted CDs, or even old socks! Be sure to ask an adult before you borrow any kitchen implements or ingredients, like pots, pans, funnels, rice, and beans. For some of the bigger tools and equipment that require adult help, such as drills, saws, screwdrivers, hammers, and glue guns, an adult will either have these at home, or be able to borrow them.

DRUM SET

What could be more fun than making music? Making the instrument to make the music, that's what! And the good news is: building yourself a drum kit is not as hard as it sounds. All you need is a few wooden poles, some buckets, a plastic bowl, a saucepan lid, and a few other things you can get in any good hardware store. You can try out different buckets and bowls for your drums, and if you feel like adding some other percussion items, you can always attach bells, tin cans, or whatever else you find. And then, drum away! You can play along to your favorite songs, or make up new beats altogether.

ABOUT THE DESIGNER

Floris Hovers is a father of four and lives in Raamsdonk, the Netherlands, where he runs a design studio. He makes lamps, chairs, and shelf units, but his favorite thing to design is wooden toy cars. When he was a child, he loved drumming on pots and plates with kitchen utensils, much to the annoyance of his neighbors. He's still not a great drummer, but he's not too bad at playing the violin!

YOU WILL NEED

(A) 11 long, thin wooden poles (2 ft 2 in x ⁵/₈ in)

(B) 1 metal saucepan lid

(C) 1 paint roller bracket with a hollow handle

(D) 2 short, thin wooden poles (14 x ⁵/₁₆ in)

(E) 3 cords with stoppers (or simple shoe laces)

(F) A drill and drill bits

(G) A pen knife

(H) 1 large wooden board (22 x 9 in)

(I) 1 small wooden board (10 x 3 ¹/₂ in)

(J) 1 empty plastic bottle

(K) A screwdriver

(L) 10 thick, strong rubber bands
(about 4 in diameter)

(M) 1 sponge

(N) 3 plastic buckets (large, medium, and small)

(O) 1 large plastic bowl

(P) 2 short, fat wooden poles (14 x 1 in)

INSTRUCTIONS

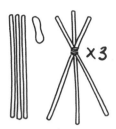

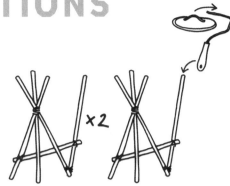

1. Tie together three of the long wooden poles with a rubber band to create a teepee, like the illustration above. Make three of these teepees.

2. Use rubber bands to attach one long wooden pole vertically and one short, thin pole horizontally (for support) to two of the teepees. Place the hollow handle of the paint roller over one of the vertical poles and hang the saucepan lid from it. Secure with a rubber band. This is your crash cymbal!

3. Cut a slit into the front of the plastic bottle with the pen knife and place it on top of the other vertical pole. This is your high drum! Place the small and medium buckets on top of your high drum and crash cymbal teepees to make your drums, and secure them to the vertical poles with two cords. Place the bowl on the last remaining teepee.

4. Tip the large bucket on its side and tie it onto the large wooden board with a cord. Ask a grown-up to drill a hole in one end of the small board and poke the pointy end of the screwdriver through it. Then place the small board onto the large board, with the screwdriver handle just behind the bottom of the bucket. Slide the sponge underneath the small board, behind the screwdriver, so that the screwdriver is at the top of the "ramp." This is your pedal. When you step on the pedal, your screwdriver will hit the bucket to make your bass drum!

5. Arrange your drum kit the way you want it to be. Pick up the two short, fat sticks — your drumsticks — and you're ready to rock and roll!

JAR IN A JAR

The most precious things are often the tiniest and easiest to lose: favorite beads, coins or marbles, pebbles from the river or shells from the beach. These glass storage jars not only help you to keep all your little treasures organized, they also let you show them off for everyone to see! All you need are some empty screw-top glass jars in a variety of sizes. The larger jar needs to be big enough for a small one to fit inside. (The easiest thing to do is to ask your parents if they can keep some empty mustard, jelly, pickle, or peanut butter jars aside for you.) Once you've constructed the Jar in a Jar, it can be used for your own little things, or given as a gift!

ABOUT THE DESIGNER

Sam Hecht set up his design studio in London with Kim Colin in 2002 and it's now one of the leading studios in the UK. Sam and his colleagues design lots of different things, such as pianos, stove tops, and toilet brushes. Although he was not very neat and organized as a child, this project was inspired by his own children, who love to store things in a nice and orderly way.

YOU WILL NEED

(A) Screw-top jars in different sizes
(B) A drill and drill bits
(C) A screwdriver

(D) Screws (max. $^3/_4 - 1$ in long) with matching wing nuts

INSTRUCTIONS

1. Choose two different-sized jars. The smaller jar should be able to fit inside the bigger one.

2. Ask a grown-up to help drill a hole in the center of each jar lid.

3. Place the small lid under the large lid, and put the screw through both lids.

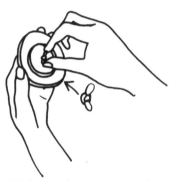

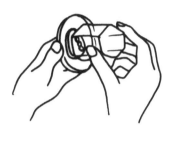

4. Twist a wing nut onto the screw to secure the two lids together.

5. Close the smaller jar with its matching lid.

6. Close the larger jar, with the smaller jar inside.

7. Fill up your jars with sweets, pocket money, shells, stones, or anything else you fancy. A beautiful way to store your treasures!

SOCK PUPPET

Socks can be tricky things, can't they? They seem to love nothing more than making a run for it whenever they can. Some get eaten up by the washing machine and others simply disappear off the face of the earth! The result? You eventually end up with a whole collection of odd socks and absolutely no idea what to do with them! Well, here's an idea: why not make them into awesome puppets? All you need are a few plastic bottles and some rice or dried beans to fill them. And if you still have lots of socks leftover, you can always make your puppet a friend or two. Bring them to life by shaking them and making rattling sounds!

ABOUT THE DESIGNER

 Jaime Hayon was born in Madrid and is one of Spain's most famous designers. His furniture and interiors can be found in design museums all over the world. He's most well-known for the playful shapes he uses in his designs: the products he makes rarely have corners or edges. This project is based on the imaginary creatures he used to make out of everyday objects when he was a child.

YOU WILL NEED

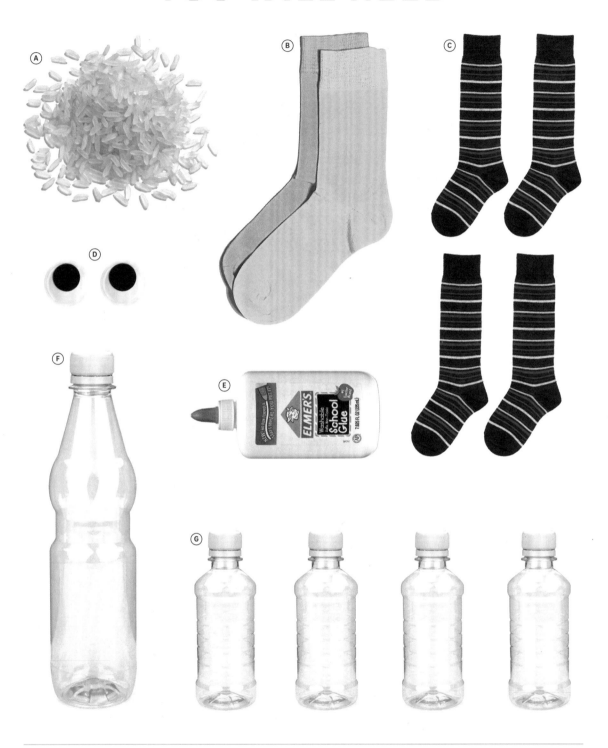

(A) Rice (or dried beans or lentils)
(B) 2 grown-ups' socks
(C) 4 long kids' socks
(D) Googly eyes

(E) Glue
(F) 1 large empty plastic bottle
(G) 4 small empty plastic bottles

INSTRUCTIONS

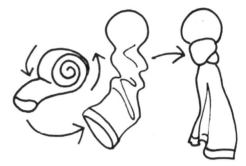

1. Fill the large bottle with a handful of rice and close it. Put the four small bottles inside the four long kid's socks.

2. To make the head, roll up one of the large socks into a ball, and stuff it into the toes of the other large sock. Tie a knot under the ball to secure it in place as the head.

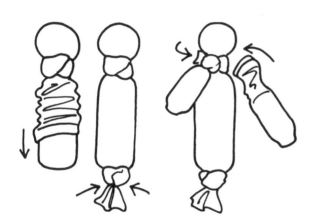

3. Put the large bottle inside the large sock, with the head at the top, and fasten the sock at the bottom with a knot. Tie two small bottles onto the neck knot to make the arms.

4. To make the legs, knot the last two small bottles to the bit of sock that's left at the bottom of the large bottle. Use glue to stick the googly eyes onto the head. Your pal is complete!

CUT & FOLD MASKS

You should always have masks at hand — for Halloween, for costume parties, for acting in plays, or for just playing around! These masks are ready to make and easy to assemble: simply print them, cut them out, and staple them together! There are four animals and four mischievous creatures to choose from. And you can make them for your whole family — they'll fit anyone, even grown-ups!

ABOUT THE DESIGNER

matali crasset spent her childhood on a farm in a village called Normée in France, where she loved building hay-bale houses. She's famous for her bright and playful designs, like these masks, which are enjoyed by children and adults alike, because they often remind adults of how they used to play as children! She's designed several hotels, a school in Brittany, furniture, kids' clothes, and even a library.

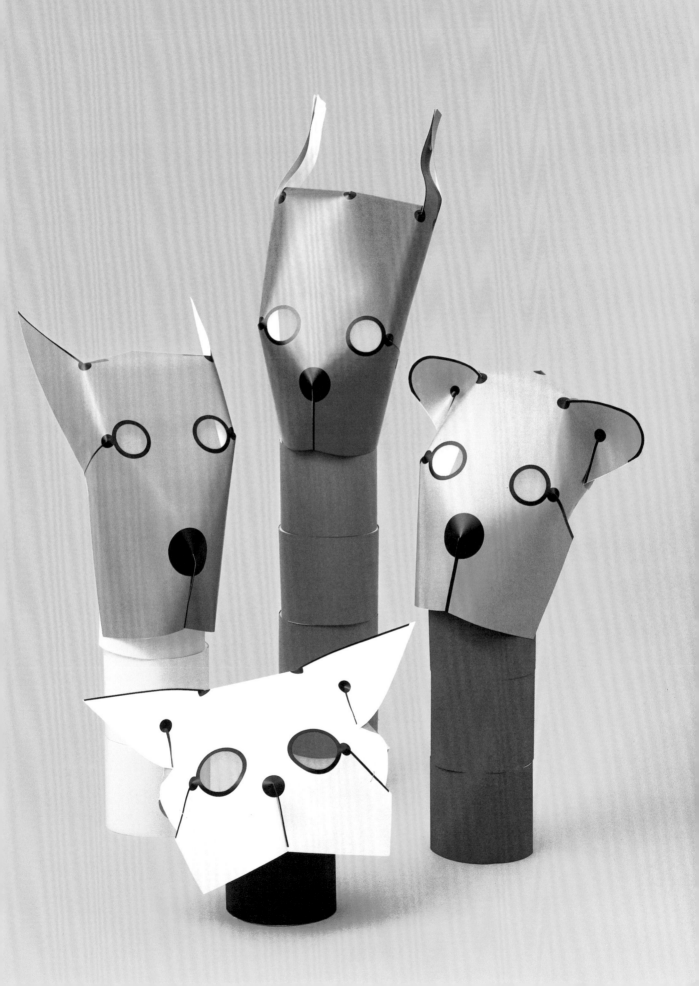

YOU WILL NEED

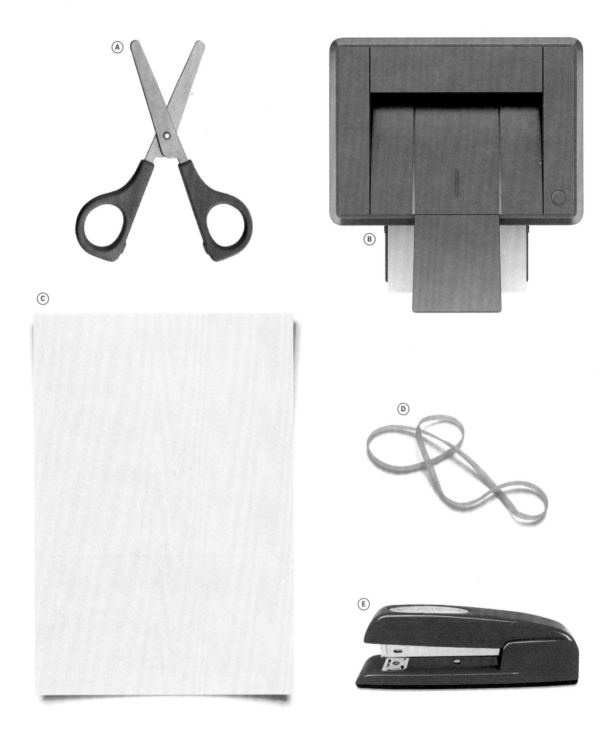

(A) Scissors
(B) A printer
(C) Thick paper or thin card

(D) A large rubber band
(E) A stapler

INSTRUCTIONS

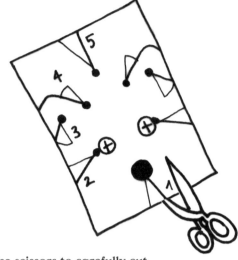

1. Print out a mask template of your choice. You can find smaller-scale examples of the masks and the web link for the full-size printable downloads on pages 106-7.

2. Use scissors to carefully cut along each numbered line, right up to the black dots, and then cut out the eyes.

3. Fold the paper to overlap the flaps made from each incision so that the shaded areas are completely covered. Once in place, staple each flap closed. This will transform your mask from flat to three-dimensional!

4. Cut a rubber band in one place so that it becomes a rubber string, and staple the ends to the left and right sides of the mask. Now your mask is ready to wear!

FAMILY MOBILE

There are lots of fun ways to decorate a room: you can hang pictures or posters on the walls, or place knick-knacks on the shelves. But what about the ceiling? Well, about a hundred years ago, an artist named Alexander Calder created the perfect decoration for ceilings when he invented the mobile, a kind of hanging sculpture that moves around in the air. This mobile, designed by Mogollon, is perfect for your home because it's made from handprints of your family's own hands! And what's more, you can take this idea and make other mobiles — with friends' hands or even with feet!

ABOUT THE DESIGNERS

Mogollon is a graphic design studio in New York. Its founders, Monica Brand and Francisco Lopez, come from Venezuela and went to art school together. Lots of their work is influenced by ancient cultures and this particular mobile was inspired by the cave paintings in the Cave of the Hands in Patagonia, which features handprints. The meaning behind the Patagonian cave paintings is yet unknown, but Mogollon likes to think that families stenciled their hands on the walls to record their time together.

YOU WILL NEED

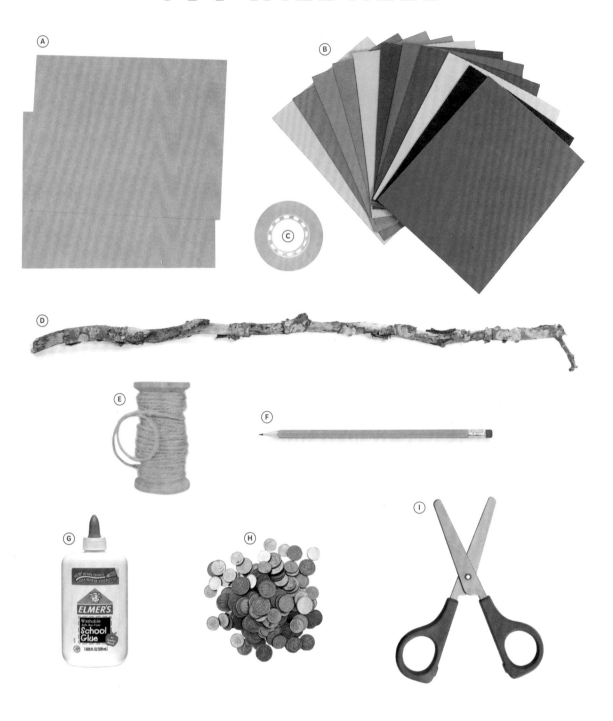

(A) Card paper or cardboard
(B) Felt in various colors, including black and white
(C) Sticky tape
(D) A nice-looking branch (about 3 ft long)

(E) 6—14 ft of string
(F) A pencil
(G) Glue
(H) Some small coins, preferably pennies
(I) Scissors

INSTRUCTIONS

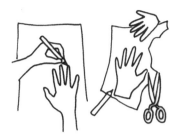

1. Trace around the hands of each member of your family on card paper and cut them out. These will be your hand templates. Trace each of the templates twice onto different colored felts, then cut them out.

2. To make the eye cloud, use the cloud template (1) on page 108. Trace it onto card paper and cut it out. Trace the card cutout twice onto some white felt and cut it out. Then trace each of the circular shapes (templates 2—6) twice on the colored felts specified and cut them out.

3. Cut the string into 4—5 pieces, each between 14—30 in long. Glue one end of a piece of string to a coin and then glue the coin onto the middle of a cloud or hand template and tape over it. Then glue a matching felt cloud or hand cutout onto the card, over the coin and string. Paste the other matching felt cloud or hand onto the other side of the card, so both sides are covered in felt. Complete the cloud by glueing eye parts on both sides.

4. Add a few other card templates (hands or clouds) onto your string by taping them in place, then glue on the matching felt pieces. Repeat steps 3 and 4 on the other pieces of string.

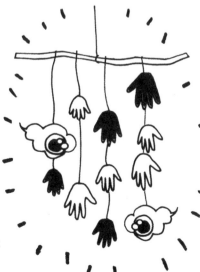

5. Tie a fresh piece of string to the middle of your branch. This is the string from which your mobile will hang.

6. Lay your branch on the floor and arrange the decorated strings along the branch. Try to balance out the weight so that when you hang the mobile, one side isn't heavier than the other. Tie the strings tightly to the branch. Now it's ready to be hung!

MARKER PEN WINDOWS

Most people think that the only purpose for windows is looking outside or letting light in. This is true, and practical, but windows can offer so much more! Think of the beautiful stained-glass windows you see in churches, mosques, synagogues, and other old buildings. Brightly colored windows can make a place look magical: red windows can make it look like the sun is setting; yellow ones can make it look sunny outside, even when it's not; and blue ones can make everything look like it's underwater. Well, you can make your own stained-glass windows using washable marker pens! They are easy to color with and to wash away, so you can change your stained-glass windows as often as you wish!

ABOUT THE DESIGNER

Helmut Smits is an artist from Rotterdam, the Netherlands. He came up with these marker pen windows during an exhibition he had in Germany. The gallery had 12 windows and he decided to buy a set of 12 coloring pens and color each window according to the order in which the pens were packed. Helmut has two kids and he loves designing children's furniture with them.

YOU WILL NEED

Ⓐ Different-colored washable marker pens

INSTRUCTIONS

1. Make sure your window is firmly shut and clean on the inside.

2. Color in the entire windowpane with a marker pen. If your window is made up of several different panes, why not color each one with a different colored pen? Your windows will look amazing! Note: only color in the glass from INSIDE your house. If you need a ladder or a chair to reach a window, ask an adult for help.

Martí Guixé

TIP TOP FLIP-FLOPS

When you go on holiday, you can usually get your flip-flops from any old beach shop. They don't cost a lot and they protect your feet from the hot sand. There's only one problem with them: everybody has the same ones! These flip-flops are 100% unique. You only need a few craft materials, and you'll have awesome-looking flip-flops before you know it! And if you'd rather not get them sandy, they make great house slippers, too.

ABOUT THE DESIGNER

 Martí Guixé is a Spanish designer who loves making everyday things — like flip-flops — just a little bit differently. For him, designing a straightforward chair or car is just not that exciting. When he first began his career as a designer, he focused on food, designing cookies with tire patterns on them, bottles with edible corks, and even angular potatoes! He has also created watches, toys, and furniture, which are all just as original as these flip-flops!

YOU WILL NEED

(A) String/cord (not too scratchy!)
(B) Cardboard
(C) Glue
(D) Felt (enough to trace your foot 4 times, and at least ¼ in thick)

(E) Scissors
(F) A pen
(G) Newspapers

INSTRUCTIONS

1. Place your feet on some cardboard, draw an oval around each foot (in the shape of a flip-flop), then cut them out with scissors.

2. Make a dot between your big toe and second toe on the cardboard cutouts, then cut slits from the top downward until you reach the dot.

3. Trace your right and left cardboard cutouts onto the felt two times each, and cut them all out. Don't forget to trace and cut the slits, too!

4. Cut a piece of string (about 4 in long) and make a knot at one end. Guide the string through the slit in the cardboard all the way up to the dot, keeping the knot underneath.

5. Lay another piece of string (about 8 in long) on the ground, and place the middle of the flip-flop and your foot on top. Bring the ends of the second string up toward your toes and tie them together, then tie the first string to them in the middle, to make your straps. Make sure your feet fit in the straps snugly, but leave a bit of space for an extra layer of felt. Trim the extra bits of strings off the knot.

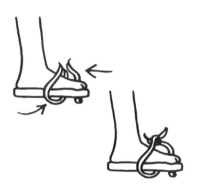

6. Stick your felt shapes on the top and bottom of each cardboard flip-flop with plenty of glue. Add glue dots or glue lines in a pattern to the very bottom of each flip-flop (on top of the felt) to create treads for traction.

7. If you like, cut out some photos or pictures from the newspapers to stick over the knots of your flip-flops with glue.

BALANCING SCULPTURE

Do you remember the first time you learned to ride a bike? It takes a while to get it right, but once you get the knack, balancing on your bike is easy! These little sculptures are exactly the same: if you find the right position for them, they will balance perfectly! Just bend the wire until you have a cool sculptural shape that balances on its own. You can even attach objects to the wire — you just need to spread the weight evenly so that it's not too heavy or too light on one side. You'll know you're finished when the sculpture stays balanced, even in a breeze!

ABOUT THE DESIGNERS

 Ladies & Gentlemen Studio is an American design studio with offices in New York and Seattle. Its founders, Dylan Davis and Jean Lee, live and work together as a design duo, creating products such as jewelry, sculptures, lighting, and furniture with stylish geometric forms made from wood, metal, and glass. This DIY project was inspired by their interest in exploring balance and movement.

YOU WILL NEED

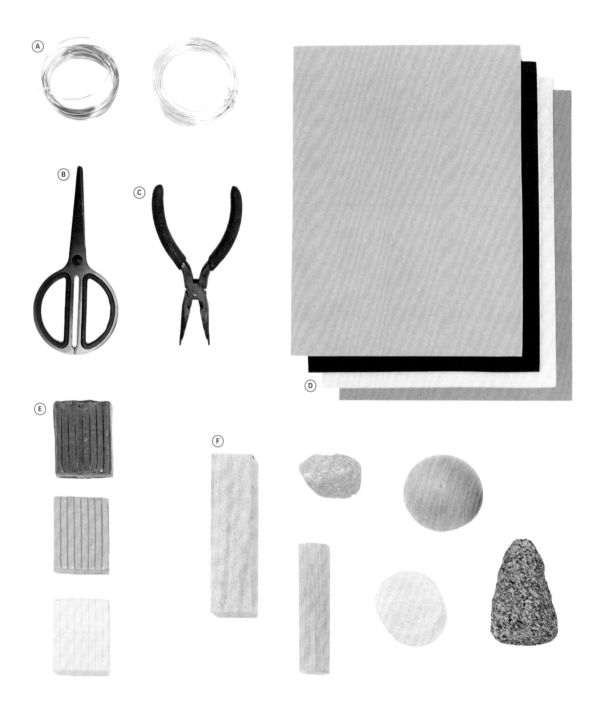

(A) Copper or aluminium modeling wire
(B) Scissors
(C) A wire cutter
(D) Lightweight foam board for modeling ($\frac{1}{4}$ in thick) in various colors

(E) Polymer modeling clay (e.g. Fimo) in various colors
(F) Pieces of wood, stones, or any other material from nature that you find suitable for the base

INSTRUCTIONS

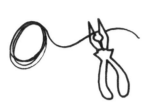

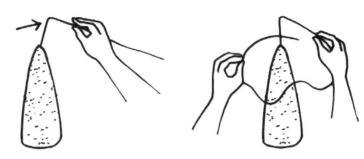

1. Measure and cut a piece of wire (about 24 — 40 in long).

2. Choose an object from nature with a flat bottom for the base. Having a little groove at the top can be helpful, too! Bend one end of your wire at an angle, and rest the end on top of your object (in the groove if there is one). This is your balancing point.

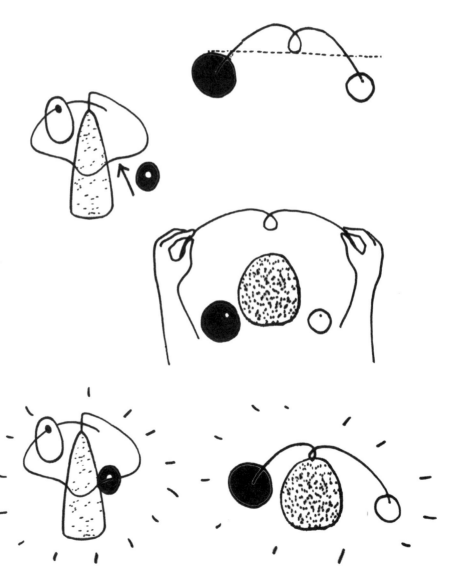

3. Mold the rest of the wire into any shape you like below your balancing point. Shape it so it balances on its own when you let go. You can also experiment by bending your wire into loops and balancing it like a seesaw.

4. Make shapes out of the polymer clay or cutouts from the soft foam board, and attach them or thread them on to the wire, making sure it can still balance on its own.

5. When you're satisfied with the sculpture and it sits sturdily, take it outside and watch it rotate in the breeze.

COST	BY	TIME
◉	Sebastian Bergne	⧗

CD SPINNER

Did you know that before the Cloud came along, people stored their digital photos, films, and music on CDs and DVDs? Today this technology is out-of-date, but there are still plenty of silver-colored plastic discs lying around, and most of them are just crying out to be recycled into something new! Ask your parents to rummage around and find you a few spare or blank CDs. With a long screw, washers, and a wing nut, you can transform them into sturdy spinning tops. Before you assemble them, decorate some CD labels with colorful, geometric patterns and stick them on the CDs so you can watch the colors and patterns blur together as they spin!

ABOUT THE DESIGNER

Sebastian Bergne was born in London and is one of the UK's leading designers. As well as designing everyday household products like cooking pots, closets, and vacuum cleaners, he also makes playful projects, like a greenhouse out of see-through Lego bricks. He thinks that the objects we fill our homes with should be a little more fun and special than what's usually sold in shops.

YOU WILL NEED

Ⓐ Old or blank CDs or DVDs

Ⓑ Colored pencils or felt-tip pens

Ⓒ White CD labels that you can draw on

Ⓓ Washers in a variety of sizes

Ⓔ Threaded roundhead screws (approx. 2—
2 ½ in long) with nuts and wing nuts to fit

INSTRUCTIONS

1. Decorate the CD labels with patterns or designs using colored pencils or felt-tip pens. Stick the labels onto the CDs.

2. To assemble a spinning top, thread items onto a screw in this order: a nut, 1–3 washers (smallest first), a CD, with its colorful side facing up, 1–3 washers (largest first), and a wing nut. Make sure that the screw and the washers are centered and straight before you tighten everything up with the wing nut.

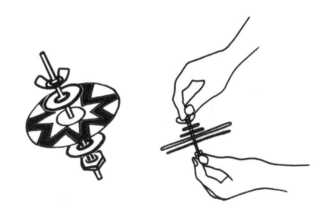

3. Place the spinner with the head of the screw on a flat surface, hold the wing nut between your fingers, and spin away!

FISHNET LAMP

Plastic bottles are a serious problem for the environment. When they are thrown away, they don't decompose, and they often end up in the ocean where they clump together with other bits of plastic to form rubbish patches sometimes as big as an entire country! Perhaps a better solution for your own empty plastic bottles is to reuse them yourself. This hanging lamp is made from plastic bottles, a pair of fishnet tights, and an LED bulb. It looks really unusual and also throws beautiful crisscross shadows onto the wall.

ABOUT THE DESIGNERS

Neri&Hu is a Chinese architecture and design studio based in Shanghai, founded by husband and wife Lyndon Neri and Rossana Hu. The pair's work usually involves redecorating restaurants and hotels and renovating old houses, but they also design furniture such as closets and dining tables. And if that doesn't sound like enough, they also run a department store and work as teachers. This lamp is a modern take on a traditional Chinese lantern.

YOU WILL NEED

(A) A glue gun
(B) Sticky tape
(C) 1 pair of fishnet tights
(D) Scissors
(E) A geometry compass
(F) Large plastic bottles of various shapes
(and colors if you like)

(G) 1 lamp fitting and cable
(H) 1 LED bulb
(I) A pencil
(J) A utility knife
(K) Soft black foam board for modeling,
or strong, black card

INSTRUCTIONS

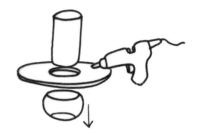

1. Slice the plastic bottles into two or three segments of different lengths. Put aside the top layer and its cap as you won't be using it.

2. Draw a few donut-shaped discs onto the foam board or card using a compass set between 3—8 ¹/₂ in (be sure they have larger diameters than your plastic bottles), and cut them out.

3. Arrange the bottle pieces and discs to make your lampshade. Start with the bottom of one of your cut bottles, then layer it with a disc and another segment of bottle. Ask a grown-up to help you glue them together with the glue gun. You can stop here or keep going until you've built a tall lampshade.

4. Trace the diameter of the top of your lampshade onto the foam twice, and cut out two discs. Cut a slit wide enough for your lamp cable to pass through from the edge to the middle in each disc. These discs will close the top of the lampshade and hold the fishnet, cable, and lamp fitting in place.

5. Cut off one leg of the fishnet tights and stretch it over the lampshade from the bottom up. Make sure the open end is at the top.

6. Ask a grown-up to help connect the lamp fitting to the bulb and feed the bulb into the lampshade. Slip one of the discs onto the cable and push it down through the top of the lampshade. Feed the remaining fishnet through the top as well, then take the second disc and slip it onto the cable and insert it on top, making sure to sandwich the remaining fishnet between it and the first disc. Push the disc down so that it's flush with the top of the lampshade. Ask your parents to help you switch on the bulb. Wow!

BERNARD THE HERMIT CRAB

Bernard the Hermit Crab was originally a homework project. A boy called Tito was asked by his teacher to make a hermit crab over the summer holidays with his family. Lucky for Tito, his dad, Giulio Iacchetti, was a designer! Together they researched hermit crabs and decided to make Bernard's legs out of little finger-shaped balloons filled with rice and his body from felt. Tito was very proud of the crab he took to school, and was excited to see that all his friends had made great-looking crabs, too! So you can build Tito's hermit crab or design and make your own!

ABOUT THE DESIGNER

Giulio Iacchetti is an Italian designer born in Castelleone. He was awarded Italy's most prestigious design prize for his famous Moscardino mini fork, which is a fork that also becomes a spoon when you turn it around! He won the prize for a second time for his Sfera manhole covers, which make everyday manhole covers both useful and really fun to look at. As well as designing cutlery, letter openers, and furniture, he has also designed a rations box for soldiers.

YOU WILL NEED

Ⓐ Felt (8 x 12 x ¹/₄ in)
Ⓑ Round self-adhesive felt pads like the ones used for the bottoms of chair legs (4 white, 2 smaller ones in black)
Ⓒ A funnel
Ⓓ Scissors
Ⓔ A pen
Ⓕ Rice
Ⓖ 5 long balloons in various colors
Ⓗ Sewing thread
Ⓘ A safety pin
Ⓙ A sewing needle

INSTRUCTIONS

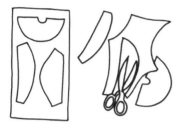
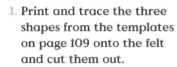

1. Print and trace the three shapes from the templates on page 109 onto the felt and cut them out.

2. Roll the semicircular felt piece into a cone and ask an adult to help sew it together. Wrap the middle-sized felt piece around this and stitch it together. Finally, wrap the long, slim felt piece around everything and stitch it on so that the three pieces form a shell house.

3. Fill five long balloons with rice using the funnel and knot them at the top.

4. Stick the safety pin through all five balloon knots and pin them together. Insert the safety pin (with the balloons) inside the cone of the shell. Make sure plenty of the hermit crab's "legs" are sticking out at the bottom, and then stitch the safety pin in place, making sure not to puncture the balloons.

5. Take two of the white round felt pads (these are the eyes), and stick the top half of each onto the bottom of the shell house. Stick the other two white felt pads in the same position from the inside. Finish the eyes by sticking the black pads on top of the white ones.

!

PROPELLER PLANE

You've probably made paper planes before, but with this one, people will surely ask you where you bought it. And you will wow them by saying, "Oh, no, I didn't buy it in a shop, I made it!" This plane, which was inspired by single-propeller planes like the famous ones built by a company called Cessna, will, of course, require a bit more time and effort than a paper plane. You'll need to saw a wooden piece, sand it down, and cut out other things, too . . . not to mention all the hammering and riveting required. It's worth the effort, though! This plane is really easy to hold, almost indestructible, and looks amazing.

ABOUT THE DESIGNER

Tomas Kral was born in Slovakia and studied in Lausanne, Switzerland, where he now runs a design studio. He designs useful and playful products, like a lamp with a shade made from a baseball cap, and a homework table with a "moat" to catch things so they don't fall off! When he was a little boy he loved watching planes take off and land at his local airport. When he was older (about 10 years old), he built his own model planes and hung them from the ceiling of his room.

YOU WILL NEED

(A) 1 piece of wood (12 x 1 ¹/₂ x 1 in)
(B) Thin, strong plastic sheets (like dividers for a filing cabinet) or strong card — in your favorite color
(C) A hammer
(D) A rivet punch to make holes
(E) Sandpaper (240 grit)
(F) 1 pearl-headed pin

(G) A pencil
(H) Scissors
(I) A utility knife
(J) A ruler
(K) A handsaw
(L) Small nails
(M) Rivets
(N) A drawing pin

INSTRUCTIONS

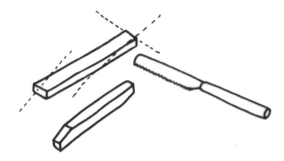

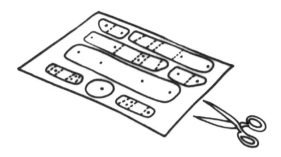

1. Print and trace template 1 on page 110 onto your piece of wood. Ask a grown-up to saw the corners off each end, following the template. Sand the surfaces with the sandpaper to make them smooth.

2. Print and trace templates 2–9 (pages 110–111) onto your plastic sheets or colored card, and cut them all out with scissors. Make sure to transfer the big and small circles from the templates, too.

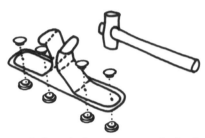

3. Ask a grown-up for help using the utility knife to carefully score along the dotted lines on pieces 3, 5, 6, 7, 8, and 9. Bend the pieces along these dotted lines to make the tail and wing parts of your plane.

4. Ask an adult to help you stamp holes into the bigger circles in your template with the rivet punch, then assemble the wings and tail, following the diagrams here, and hammer them together with the rivets.

5. Following the smaller circles in the template, ask an adult to help you use four nails to hammer the wings, and four nails to hammer the tail to the body of the plane. Punch a hole using the rivet punch in the propeller piece 4 and fasten it to the plane using the pearl-headed pin. Push the drawing pin into the front of your plane, just under the wings: this is the pilot!

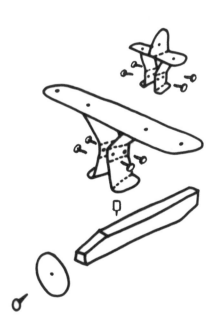

ROLL-O ROOM DIVIDER

Wouldn't it be handy to be able to divide a room in half, or better yet — to make a room within a room? Well, all you need is this room divider! You can build a wall so tall that you are completely hidden from others, or you can build yourself a cozy den where you can hang out without being disturbed. It's super easy to make, and the best bit is that it's totally adaptable: you can make it as high or as wide as you want! All you need is a bunch of toilet rolls, some sticky tape, and some colorful paper!

ABOUT THE DESIGNER

 Julia Hasting was born in Bremen, Germany, and lives and works in Zurich, Switzerland. She is the Creative Director at the publishing house Phaidon (the publishers of this book!), and her job is to make sure that all their books look and feel their best. She often designs them herself, creating beautiful covers and page designs. In her spare time, Julia likes coming up with DIY projects like this one with her two children, who happened to share a room for many years!

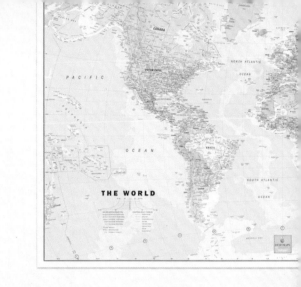

YOU WILL NEED

Ⓐ A variety of colored paper

Ⓑ Hair pins

Ⓒ A pencil

Ⓓ Wooden sticks or poles (optional), about
$^5/_{16}$ in wide, and as long as your wall height

Ⓔ Double-sided sticky tape

Ⓕ Scissors

Ⓖ Lots of toilet rolls (number depends
on the size of your wall)

Ⓗ A ruler

INSTRUCTIONS

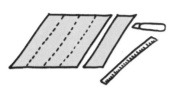
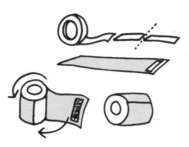

1. Measure the height and the circumference of one of your toilet rolls and add 1 in to the circumference. Use these measurements to cut your colored paper into strips (circumference = length).

2. Stick a strip of double-sided sticky tape to both short ends of the paper and wrap it around the toilet roll, sticking the first end to the toilet paper, and the other end to the paper itself. Do the same with all your toilet rolls so that they are all covered in color!

3. Decide what shape you want your wall to be. For example, do you want it to be straight or curved? Then place the first row of toilet rolls where you want your room divider to begin.

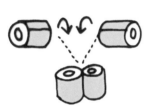

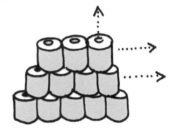

4. Place the toilet rolls so that the ends of the colored paper covers are touching one another (that way the edges won't show from the outside).

5. Attach the toilet rolls together using the hair pins by sticking them into the toilet paper.

6. For the second and third layers, stagger the rolls like bricks, so that one rolls sits on top of where the two underneath it meet. Build your wall as tall and wide as you like!

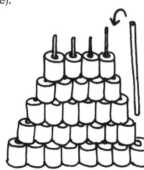

7. For extra sturdy walls, you can use long wooden sticks or poles. The sticks should be dropped into the holes of the top layer of toilet rolls, then (because the rows are staggered) they go between the two rolls underneath it, and then through the holes of the third layer of toilet rolls, and so on, until the sticks are invisible.

CLAY LAMP

You've probably seen all kinds of lamps in homes and in shops, but have you ever wondered how you could make your own lamp look exactly the way you want it to? This lampstand is actually a clay sculpture, which means it can be molded into any shape you want it to be! Can you imagine your bedside lamp being your favorite animal, food, or movie character? You could even make a lampstand out of your initials!

ABOUT THE DESIGNERS

Front is a design studio based in Stockholm, Sweden, set up by design duo Anna Lindgren and Sofia Lagerkvist. They are famous for their unusual and sometimes crazy-looking designs, like a coat stand made out of upside-down hangers, rugs with colorful scribbles all over them, and a lamp with a large horse-shaped stand. The horse lamp was the inspiration behind this clay lamp project. The thing that Anna and Sofia love most about their jobs is that they get to imagine and create just as they did when they were children.

YOU WILL NEED

(A) Air-drying soft clay or school clay (you can
even make your own salt-dough clay, if you
like: you can find lots of recipes for it online!)

(B) Sticky tape (optional)

(C) An old lampstand from a second-hand shop
or found lying around your house (not in use)

(D) 1 lightbulb

(E) A knife

(F) Acrylic paints

(G) 1 lamp fitting and cable

(H) 1 lampshade (optional)

INSTRUCTIONS

1. To set up the lamp, ask an adult to help you feed the cable through the lamp stand, and connect it to your lightbulb. Alternatively you can stick the cable onto the outside of the lampstand with sticky tape.

2. Use the clay to make a sculpture that is the same height as your lampstand. Don't make it higher, as you don't want it to get in the way of your bulb and (optional) lampshade!

3. Use the knife to cut an opening down the back of your sculpture so you can slot the lampstand inside.

4. Close the opening at the back of your sculpture with more clay and leave it to dry. Once it's dry, you can paint your sculpture. If you want to, place a lampshade on top. Now it's ready to plug in and switch on!

NOTE: You can also make this lamp without a metal stand: just place the lamp cable inside the clay and mold the clay so that it holds the lamp fitting at the top in place.

SITTING STOOL

There are so many different types of chairs that we see every day: upholstered armchairs that are soft and cozy, office swivel chairs that are structured and adjustable, or stools that are small and backless. Most of these demand some pretty advanced building skills, but this stool can be made by anyone! It's made from 12 planks of wood, which can be assembled with very simple joints. If you'd like a colorful stool, you can paint your wood with colored stains before you put the stool together. And if you're feeling inspired, you can even make a little table to go with it. Simply make the feet a little longer, and the seat a little bigger and you've done it!

ABOUT THE DESIGNER

 Martino Gamper is an Italian designer and artist who lives and works in London. He loves stools and chairs, and in 2007, he decided to build 100 different chairs over the course of 100 days. Some of them were made from recycled pieces of unwanted chairs he found in the street or in friends' homes. These 100 chairs have been shown in museums, and there's even a book about them.

YOU WILL NEED

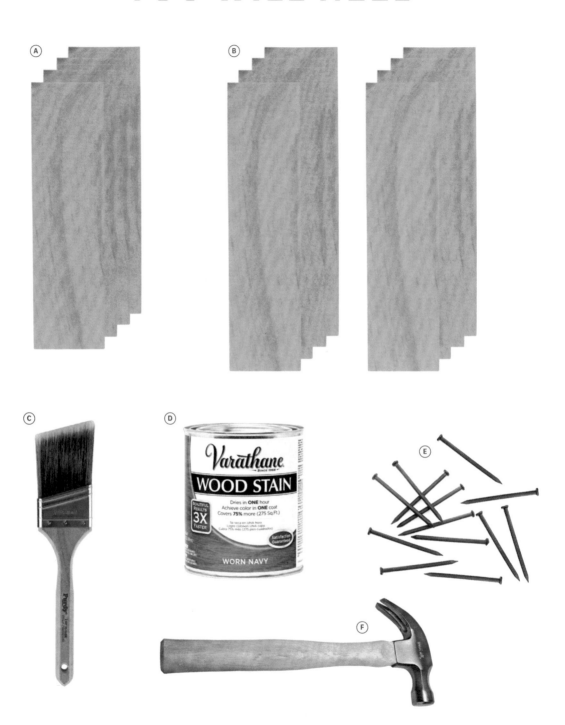

(A) 4 short wooden planks (14 x 4 x ³/₄ in)
(B) 8 longer wooden planks (14 ¹/₂ x 4 x ³/₄ in)
(C) A paintbrush (optional)

(D) Wood stain (optional)
(E) Nails (about 1 ¹/₂ in long)
(F) A hammer

INSTRUCTIONS

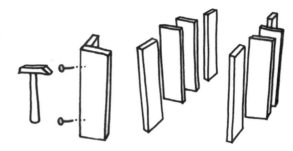

1. If you want a colorful stool, paint the planks with a colored wood stain on both sides and leave them to dry.

2. Ask a grown-up to help you nail the four shorter planks into two L-shapes and nail the eight longer planks into four L-shapes.

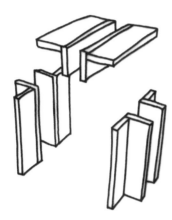

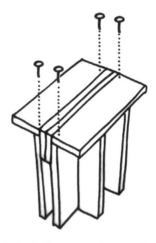

3. Assemble the stool as shown in this drawing, using the two shorter L-shapes as the stool's top.

4. Ask for help to hammer four nails through the top of the stool into the legs, as shown.

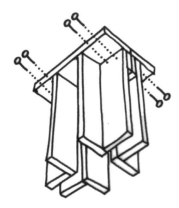

5. Hammer eight more nails into the legs just below the seat, as shown. Your stool is complete!

MAGIC MIRROR

Fairy tales aren't the only place you'll find magic mirrors. When placed at the right angle, this mirror will make it look like you have five times more money or sweets than you actually have! It can also create symmetrical patterns just like the ones you see in kaleidoscopes. The mirror is made from two equal-sized mirrors hinged together by fabric in the shape of an open book. You can play with opening it just a little wider or narrower to see different reflections!

ABOUT THE DESIGNER

Louise Campbell was born in Copenhagen, Denmark, and has loved making things for as long as she can remember. She is famous for her playful designs, such as a set of candleholders that can be clipped together in different arrangements and an armchair shaped like a flower. She is inspired by the many different patterns she finds in the world, and hopes this mirror will be something that inspires you, too!

YOU WILL NEED

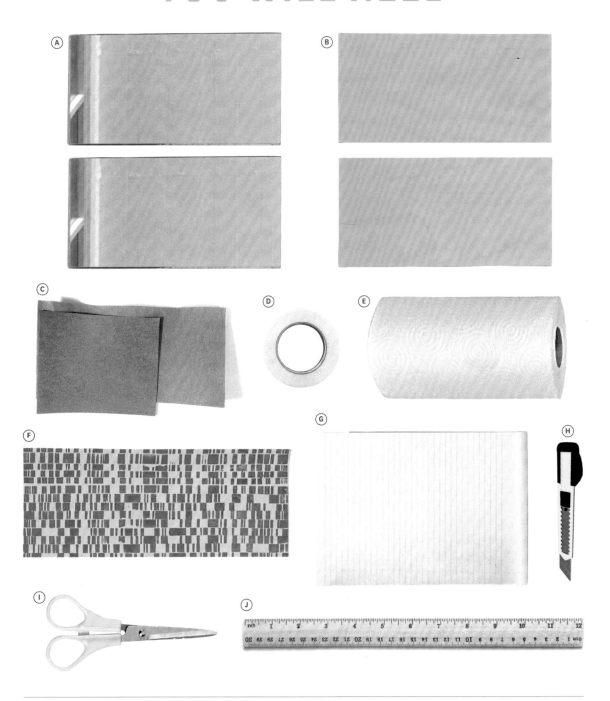

(A) 2 pieces of mirror with deburred edges
    (6 x 12 x $^{1}/_{16}$ in)
(B) 2 pieces of wood veneer, e.g., birch
    (6 x 12 x $^{11}/_{16}$ in)
(C) Fine sandpaper
(D) Double-sided sticky tape (wide)
(E) Paper towel

(F) Sturdy, non-stretchy fabric (measuring
    at least 12 x 2 $^{1}/_{2}$ in)
(G) A notepad
(H) A utility knife
(I) Scissors
(J) A ruler

INSTRUCTIONS

1. Sand down the edges of your wooden panels so they are smooth. Cover one side of a piece of wood with double-sided sticky tape and carefully attach a mirror. Make sure it is firmly stuck down. Repeat with your second piece of wood.

2. Place a piece of paper towel on top of a mirrored panel, then place the other panel on top of it, with the mirror facing down, so you have two mirrors facing each other with a piece of paper towel sandwiched between them for protection.

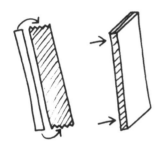

3. Stick a 12 in strip of double-sided sticky tape onto your fabric. Then stick and fold the fabric along one side of the long edges of both wooden panels to hinge them together. Cut off any excess fabric. Your mirrored panels should now open like a book.

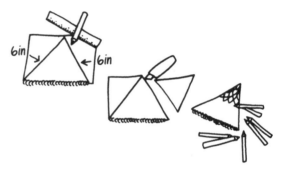

4. Ask an adult to cut the notepad into a triangle with equal sides (6 x 6 x 6 in, with 60 degrees at each corner) with the utility knife. You can find the template for this on page 112.

5. Stick a printout of one of the patterns from page 112 or draw something on the triangle notepad. Position your mirror around the triangle and prepare to be amazed!

DADA SCULPTURES

Building blocks almost always come in geometric shapes like squares and rectangles, which are great for making castles and houses, but harder for sculpting things like animals and plants. DADA blocks, on the other hand, offer irregular shapes, which give you a variety of options when building things. In fact, the name DADA comes from the Korean word for "variety"! To make a DADA sculpture, all you need are a few DADA blocks (which are easy to make), fastening straps or elastic bands, and most important of all: things you like from the forest or your garden, like feathers, flowers, twigs, and pine cones. Let your imagination run wild, and marvel at the beautiful sculptures you make!

ABOUT THE DESIGNER

Myungsik Jang is a young industrial designer from Seoul in South Korea. He invented DADA sculptures as a part of his university degree, and won an important design competition with them. When he was a child, Jang used to collect stones to create castles and animals. He loved using natural everyday objects to build things, and this inspired him to design his DADA blocks.

YOU WILL NEED

Ⓐ Wooden blocks (of different sizes and smaller than your hands)
Ⓑ A file
Ⓒ A saw
Ⓓ Sandpaper of various grits
Ⓔ A gimlet
Ⓕ Rubber bands
Ⓖ String
Ⓗ Cord stoppers
Ⓘ Grasses
Ⓙ Pine cones
Ⓚ Stones
Ⓛ Feathers
Ⓜ Leaves

INSTRUCTIONS

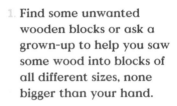

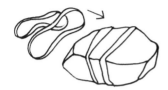

1. Find some unwanted wooden blocks or ask a grown-up to help you saw some wood into blocks of all different sizes, none bigger than your hand.

2. Ask a grown-up to help you saw, file, and sand down the hard edges of your blocks to make irregular shapes, with many sides and angles.

3. Stretch rubber bands around the largest blocks.

4. Make holes in the blocks by twisting the gimlet into them. Choose some of the blocks to make shallow holes and other blocks to make a pair of deep holes that go right through the wood so the string can be threaded through and tied. Thread cord stoppers onto the string to make loops.

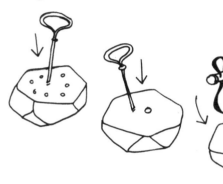

5. Use a few objects from nature, such as grass, pine cones, stones, feathers, or leaves, to turn your wooden blocks into little sculptures! Place the feathers and leaves into the small holes. Thread larger items through the rubber bands and string. Then stack up your pieces and attach together with the remaining rubber bands and string.

COPTERS

These copters are the simplest flying objects you can make from paper — you don't even have to fold them! Because of their unique shape, these copters spin to the ground like a spinning top. Try experimenting with different types of paper or different strip widths and watch how their flight changes! If you use colored paper or you color in your copters, they will look even more exciting as they fly.

ABOUT THE DESIGNER

 Christian Haas grew up in the Bavarian countryside in Germany, where he spent a lot of time with his friends competing to build the best flying objects. Whoever could keep their object in the air for the longest would win! He became a designer when he grew up, and enjoys designing artistic vases for dinner tables, chic dinnerware, attractive carafes, and glasses.

YOU WILL NEED

(A) Plain or colored paper
(B) A stapler
(C) Scissors

(D) Glue
(E) A ruler

INSTRUCTIONS

1. Photocopy or print out the templates on page 113 onto some plain or colored paper.

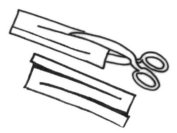

2. Choose one patterned strip, and follow the thick outlines to cut it out.

3. Cut along the two thick lines inside each strip so that you end up with a flappy piece on each side.

4. Make a triangle by lifting up the flappy ends to meet at the top. Staple these two ends together. This is the basic copter shape.

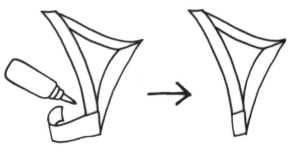

5. Cut a narrow strip of paper from a leftover scrap.

6. Glue one end of the strip right on top of the staple, and wrap the rest of the strip around and around the staple until it runs out. (It should wrap around at least three times.) Glue down the end.

7. Fly your copter by dropping it from a balcony, from the banister over a staircase, or find a tall person to drop it from above – and watch it spin!

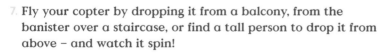

PLASTIC PAL

Have you noticed how much plastic we use every day? So many of the products we buy come in plastic containers and our kitchens are full of plastic bottles, whether they're for dishwashing liquid, cleaning detergent, water, or milk. You can recycle most bottles, but you can also use a few of them to make this plastic pal — your little bottle buddy. And because there are all kinds of plastic bottles to choose from, your plastic pals will never look completely alike. Why not make one as a mascot for your sports club or band, or use one as a scarecrow in your garden?

ABOUT THE DESIGNER

Stephen Burks is one of America's groundbreaking designers and has a design studio in New York. He enjoys collaborating with craftspeople from all over the world to make unique handmade products. Through these collaborative projects, he helps to preserve these artisans' working methods and traditions while protecting the environment. He loves using would-be throwaways to make exciting new things — just like this funny pal!

YOU WILL NEED

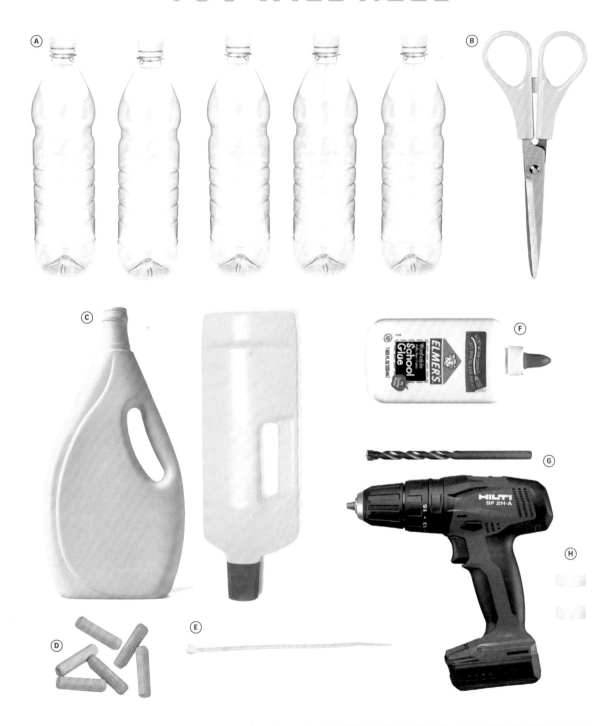

Ⓐ 5 small plastic water bottles (empty)

Ⓑ Scissors

Ⓒ 2 larger plastic bottles (detergent or household cleaner bottles—empty)

Ⓓ 6 wooden dowels

Ⓔ 1 cable tie

Ⓕ Glue

Ⓖ A drill and drill bit (the same diameter as the dowels)

Ⓗ 2 spare bottle caps

INSTRUCTIONS

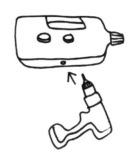

1. Glue the two spare plastic bottle caps onto the top of the larger bottle you wish to use as the head: these are the eyes.

2. Ask an adult to help you with the drilling. Drill a hole into the center of this bottle where you would like it to join to the body.

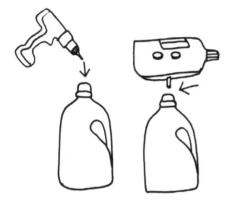

3. Drill another hole into the center of the cap of the other large bottle, which you will use for the body. Push a wooden dowel halfway into that hole, and then attach the head to the body by pushing its hole onto the dowel.

4. Drill holes into the bottoms of two smaller bottles for the arms, and drill holes into the body where you want the arms to be. Attach with dowels, as in step 3.

5. Drill holes into the caps of three smaller bottles for the legs and insert three dowels. Tie the bottles together at the top with a cable tie so that they form a stable standing pyramid. Put on the caps with the dowels. Mark where the 3 dowels of the pyramid will sit on the bottom of the body and drill 3 holes to the body, then attach the legs. Well, hello there!

BOOK SHELF

As you get older you lose interest in reading the books you loved when you were little . . . but you can't bear to give them away! First, they get dusty sitting on the shelf, then they get moved into the basement or the attic. Well, here's a way to keep those books nearby and perfectly intact: use them to build shelves for your room! All you need are some clips and rope. The best books to use are stiff, hardback ones. The shelf can be hung on the wall or from the ceiling and you can easily add new shelves when you need them. And whenever you want to look through your beloved old books again, just take them down and swap them for other ones!

ABOUT THE DESIGNER

Werner Aisslinger was born in Nördlingen, Germany. Before he set up his own design studio, he worked for several famous designers. He now designs furniture, appliances, and various kinds of interiors, and has been awarded many prizes. This bookshelf was originally created for a futuristic house designed by Werner called "House of Wonders". It was housed in a room full of books called "chamber of books". He believes that books will always remain an important part of our lives.

YOU WILL NEED

Ⓐ Binder clips (4 per book)
Ⓑ Colored rope (approx. 16 ft length required for 4 books, ¹/₄ in thick)

Ⓒ Old children's books (not too thick, all of a similar size, hardback covers).

INSTRUCTIONS

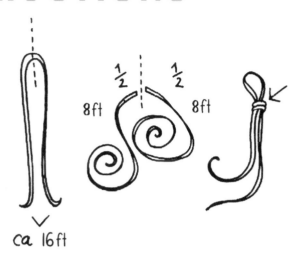

ca 16ft

1. Clip two binder clips onto the short sides of each of your books, as shown.

2. Cut your rope exactly in half so you have two pieces of rope the same length. Fold each length of rope in half and tie a knot near the top, leaving a loop for hanging. You now have two sets of loops with two hanging ropes to which you can attach your shelves.

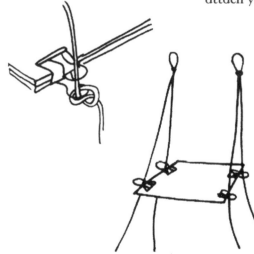

3. Start with the smallest book (this will be your top shelf). Use one set of hanging ropes, and thread the ropes through the two clips on one side of the book. Tie a knot around the lower metal part of each clip to secure it in place. Repeat this with the other set of loops and strings for the other side of the book, making sure the shelf is level before tying the knots. Once the top book is threaded in all four places, continue downwards with the other shelves. Make sure you leave the same amount of rope between each knot, so that the shelves are level!

4. Ask an adult for help mounting your hanging shelves to the wall or to the ceiling.

CRITTERS

Do you have a favorite pair of shoes that are super comfortable but are looking a bit worn and scruffy? You can bring any old shoes back to life (or transform any ordinary lace-ups) by adding a few simple pieces of leather and making these fabulous Critters: friendly creatures with floppy ears, that snuggle up on your feet and stick their tongues out at the world.

ABOUT THE DESIGNER

 Rodrigo Almeida is a Brazilian designer and artist who lives in São Paulo. Many of his imaginative products, such as his chairs, are one-offs, which means there's only one in the whole world. He likes to use items that he finds in markets, second-hand shops, and DIY shops such as fabrics, miscellaneous oddities, nylon cords, and bits of leather. When he was a child he liked to use toys and household objects to create stories and characters. He hopes that you can do the same with these Critters!

YOU WILL NEED

Ⓐ Scissors
Ⓑ A pencil
Ⓒ At least 2 pieces of thin leather (more for multicolored Critters, approx. 8 x 10 in)

Ⓓ A pair of lace-up shoes
Ⓔ A hole punch

INSTRUCTIONS

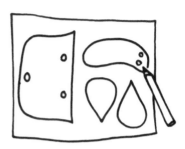

1. Print and trace the shapes from the templates on page 118 onto your leather pieces, adapting the size of the shapes according to your shoe size. (Make sure they're the same size for both shoes.)

2. Cut out all the shapes with scissors and open the holes with the hole punch.

3. Pull out the laces from one of your shoes. Run the lace through the holes of the tongue, and then lace up the first holes in your shoe. Proceed with lacing your shoe as normal to the top. Place the Critter's face on top of the shoe and run the laces through the holes in its face and then ears. Now do the same with the other shoe.

4. Pull the laces tight so that your shoes fit comfortably, and then fix the leather pieces in place with a knot. If there is any extra lace left, you can cut it off or simply tuck it back inside your shoes.

CANDY LAMP

This project shows you just what you can create from some very simple materials. It doesn't involve much more than using a template, cutting a pattern, and tying it together. When you complete it, you get a twisted structure that looks like candy! With a little help from an adult, you can attach it to a light fitting to make an elegant hanging lamp, or you can make a smaller, unlit ornament. Both are unique and beautiful, and will make you think of sweets!

ABOUT THE DESIGNER

Elise Fouin is a designer from Paris, France. The pieces she designs are often described as having a certain poetry to them: from a wooden wall lamp that resembles a flying kite to a hanging wire mesh lamp that looks like a butterfly. She particularly likes working with paper, which is a simple material that always inspires her to create unusual objects.

YOU WILL NEED

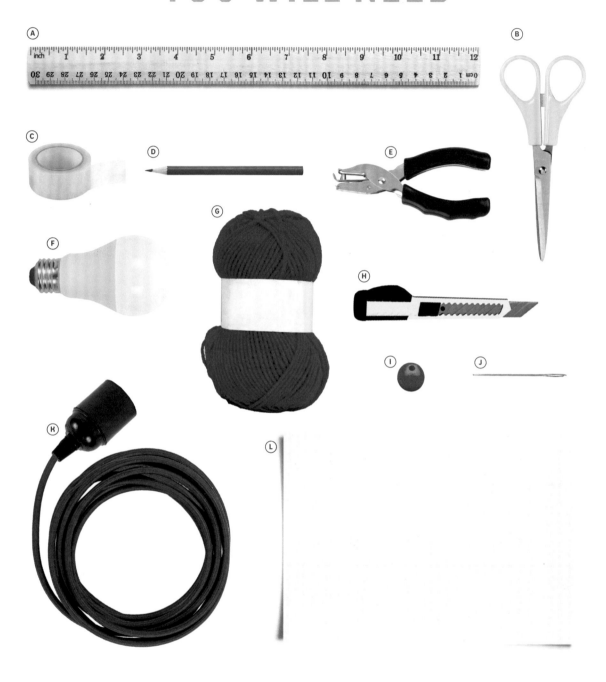

(A) A ruler
(B) Scissors
(C) Transparent sticky tape
(D) A pencil
(E) Hole punch pliers
(F) 1 LED light bulb
(G) 7 feet of wool yarn

(H) A utility knife
(I) 1 wooden bead
(J) A large sewing needle
(K) 1 light fitting and cable
(L) Paper (E size — 34 x 44 in — for a hanging
     lampshade, tabloid size for an ornament)

INSTRUCTIONS

1. To make the lamp, print the template on page 115 at a copy shop, enlarged to size E paper (34 x 44 in), or replicate it with a pencil and ruler on a piece of size E paper using the measurements given. To make the smaller, unlit ornament, follow the instructions on page 116.

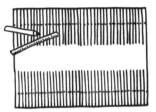

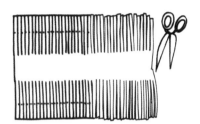

2. Punch small holes through the points marked on the template with the hole punch pliers.

3. Cut along the solid lines to make parallel strips along each side of the paper.

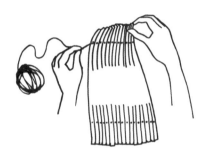

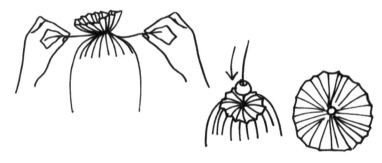

4. Cut approximately 3 ft of yarn, thread the needle with it, and thread it through the holes in each strip, from left to right, according to the instructions on page 114.

5. The threaded paper strips should form a kind of bowl. Tie both ends of the yarn together in a knot. The bottom of your lamp will look like a round fan. Thread the wool through the wooden bead so that it sits outside the bottom of your lamp and secure it with another knot.

6. Ask a grown-up to help you assemble the lightbulb fitting and cable, and lay the light fitting inside the paper lampshade, as shown in the picture above.

7. Repeat step 4 along the strips on the other side until the lampshade has closed up around the light cable, and tie the yarn together with a knot. Close up the open side of the lamp with a piece of transparent sticky tape. Ask an adult to help you hang it up and turn the light on.

MAGIC CABINET

This little wooden cabinet is perfect for hiding away your precious, secret things. Diaries, maps, and lucky charms — things that are for your eyes only! The cabinet may not look all that special from the outside, but it has an invisible lock, which can only be opened with a special magnetic key if you know where the hidden hinge is. The cabinet also has wheels so you can move it anywhere you like — even next to your bed, for example, as a bedside table. A pretty good disguise in itself!

ABOUT THE DESIGNER

Elia Mangia has a design studio in Milan, Italy, where he lives and works. When he was a child he had a lot of trouble protecting his most precious things from his big brother and so when he grew up he created this magic vault, which he thinks would have made his life much easier! Today, he designs all sorts of objects, from furniture to hair dryers. His favorite part of designing is when he gets to build!

YOU WILL NEED

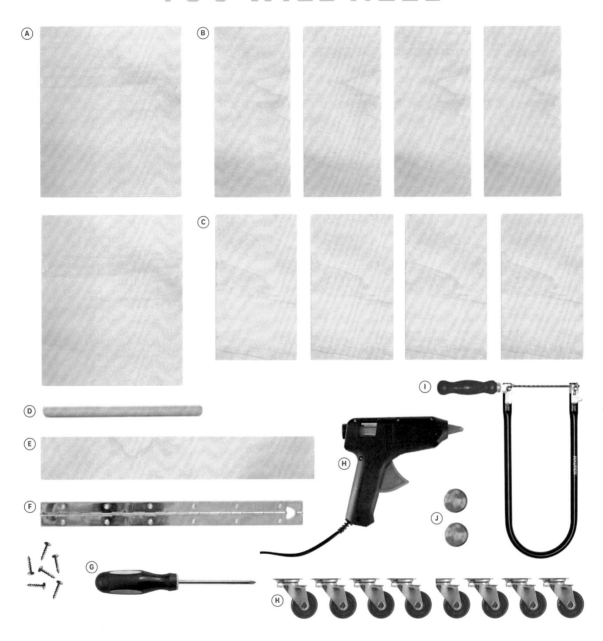

(A) 2 plywood panels (16 $\frac{1}{2}$ x 14 x $\frac{5}{8}$ in)
(B) 4 plywood panels (16 $\frac{1}{2}$ x 8 x $\frac{5}{8}$ in)
(C) 4 plywood panels (14 x 8 $\frac{1}{4}$ x $\frac{5}{8}$ in)
(D) 1 round wooden pole (4 x 1 in)
(E) 1 thin wooden slat (4 x 19 $\frac{1}{2}$ x $\frac{5}{16}$ in)
(F) 1 hinge strip (at least 12 in long) and screws to fit
(G) A screwdriver
(H) A glue gun
(I) A coping saw

(J) 2 round magnets
(K) 8 castor wheels (1 $\frac{1}{2}$ in diameter)

INSTRUCTIONS

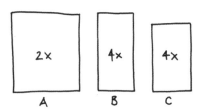

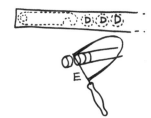

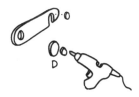

1. Buy specially cut panels of plywood to the measurements in the materials list. We will refer to these panels as (A), (B), and (C), as above.

2. Print and trace the latch and disc templates on page 119 onto the thin wooden slat. Ask a grown-up to cut out the latch and the three D discs with a saw, and saw two E discs, each 1/2 in thick, from the round pole.

3. Ask a grown-up to help glue one magnet onto the latch as shown and the other to one of the D discs: this D disc will be your key when opening the cabinet.

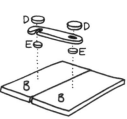

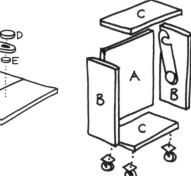

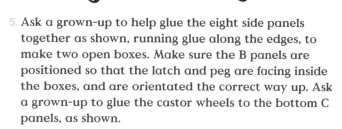

4. Lay two B panels side by side, leaving a gap of 1/8 in between them and place the latch down to mark where the hinge and hook should go. Make sure there is space for the latch to swing up without hitting the top of the cabinet. Ask a grown-up to help glue the E discs in place as shown, then the two remaining D discs on top of them.

5. Ask a grown-up to help glue the eight side panels together as shown, running glue along the edges, to make two open boxes. Make sure the B panels are positioned so that the latch and peg are facing inside the boxes, and are orientated the correct way up. Ask a grown-up to glue the castor wheels to the bottom C panels, as shown.

6. Connect the two boxes together by screwing the hinge strip along the open edges of the two B panels that don't have the latch and peg, so that when you swing it closed, the latch and peg will meet. Place the things you want to keep secret inside, and use the magnet disc key to open!

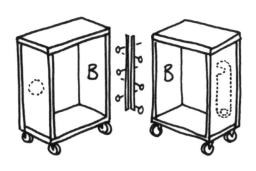

PLAYHOUSE

Who doesn't love grabbing a bunch of chairs, blankets, and cushions to build a fort? If only you didn't have to put everything back where it belonged! Well, with this project, you don't have to take it down because you don't use any furniture! All you need is cardboard boxes, tape, scissors, and your inner architect! Let your imagination run wild: it's up to you to decide where the windows, doors, and skylights will be. Keep a few boxes open, facing both inside and outside, to use as storage shelves for things like books, toys, and lamps. You can even add color or decoration to the boxes as finishing touches!

ABOUT THE DESIGNERS

There's barely anything that Mårten Claesson, Eero Koivisto, and Ola Rune haven't designed yet, from toothbrushes, smartphones, and colorful furniture, to futuristic apartment blocks. Their Stockholm design studio, Claesson Koivisto Rune, is one of the most prestigious in Sweden. This playhouse is especially important to them, as Eero built about 50 mini houses like this one when he was a child!

YOU WILL NEED

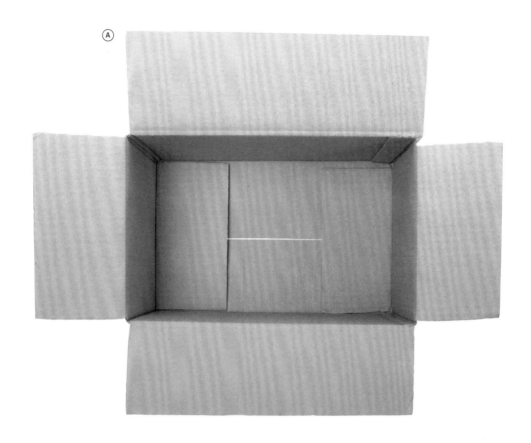

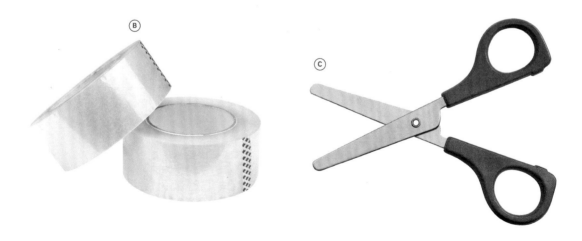

(A) 20—40 cardboard packing boxes of the same size (24 x 18 x 12 in, for example)

(B) Packing tape
(C) Scissors

INSTRUCTIONS

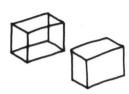

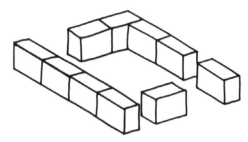

1. Assemble your boxes and tape them closed. Leave a few boxes open on one side by folding the flaps into the box. These can be used as shelves or storage.

2. Start with the bottom layer of your house. Lay your boxes down in a large rectangle shape, with space in the middle. Remove a few of them so there are some gaps. These gaps will be your doorways! Connect the boxes to each other with packing tape for stability (it works well to run tape across two or three boxes together).

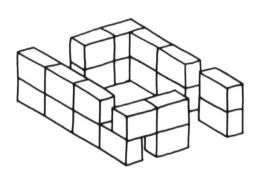

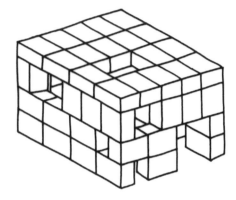

3. Stack another row of boxes on top of your first ones, again taping blocks together and to the row below, leaving gaps above the doorway, as well as extra gaps for windows. You can stop here, or, for bigger houses, add a third and fourth layer.

4. For your ceiling, count the number of boxes along the short side of your house, and create another line of boxes of the same amount plus one extra on each end. Tape them together width-wise, and then lay them across the top of your walls. Repeat until your entire roof is covered, leaving a few spaces empty for skylights!

5. Decorate and fill the shelves with your favorite things.

TEM
PLA
TES

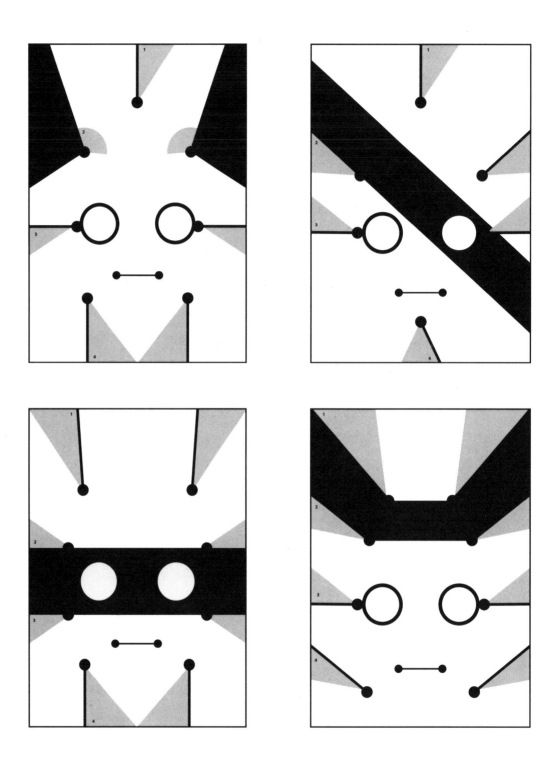

Here are the mask templates for four mischievous pals and four animals to choose from. You can print out the full-size mask templates from www.phaidon.com/NMT

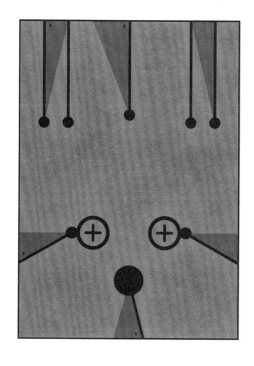 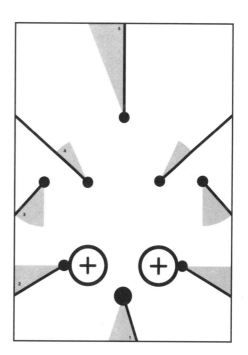

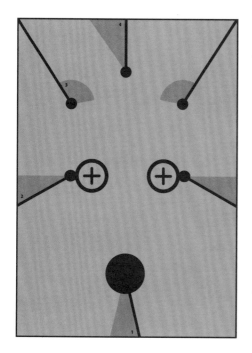 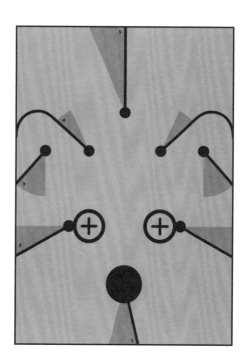

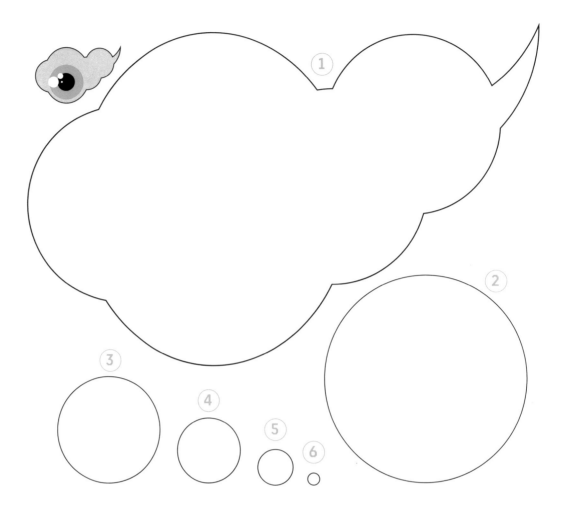

The eye cloud is made from the following pieces:

1 Cloud shape (use white felt)

2 Iris (the colored part of the eye, so use blue, green, brown, or gray felt)

3 Pupil (the black part in the middle of the eye, so use black felt)

4 5 6 Reflections in the eye (use white felt)

Photocopy these at 200% (two times their size) or print out the shapes from www.phaidon.com/NMT so they can be cut out and transferred onto your felt pieces.

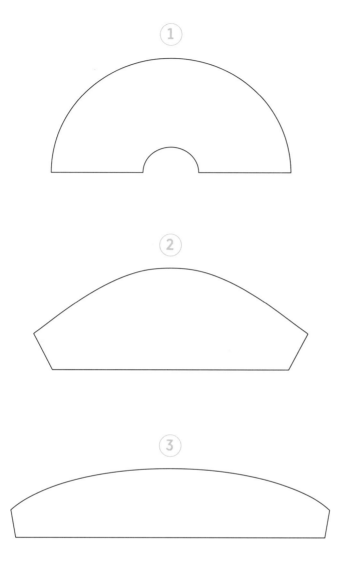

① ② ③

Bernard the Hermit Crab's body is made from these three shapes. Photocopy the shapes at 200% (two times their size) or print them out from www.phaidon.com/NMT, and cut them out. Trace your cutouts onto your felt pieces and then cut them out.

Print out these templates from www.phaidon.com/
NMT, then cut them out and tape or paste them
onto your wood and plastic sheets or strong cards.
If you trace them, don't forget to trace the holes
and dotted lines as well!

Template 1 is a side view of the plane's wooden
body (fuselage). You should only have to trace the
diagonal line at the top left corner and bottom
right corner. The dotted lines show you where the
wings and tail are going to be attached.

Transfer the templates for the wings (2), tail fins (6,
9), propeller (4), and support struts (3, 5, 7, 8) onto
plastic sheets or strong cards and cut them out.

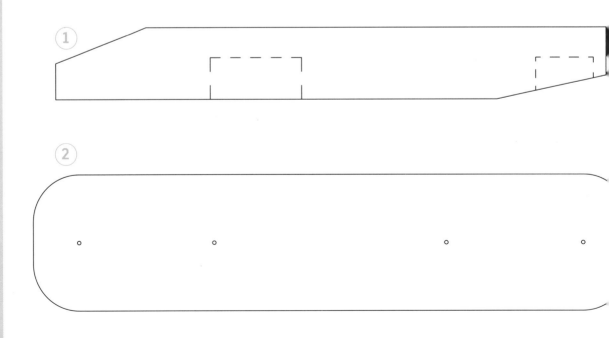

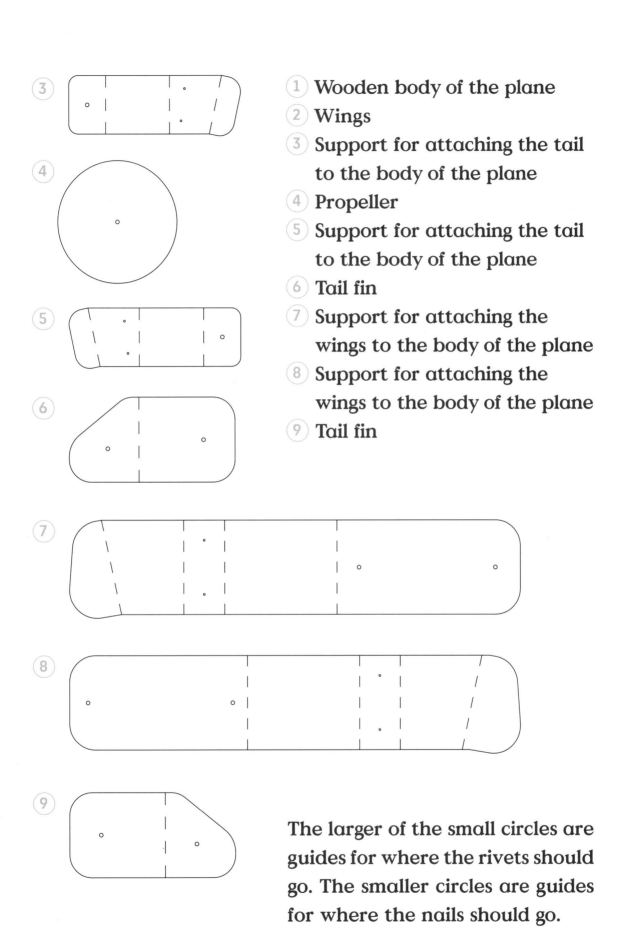

1. Wooden body of the plane
2. Wings
3. Support for attaching the tail to the body of the plane
4. Propeller
5. Support for attaching the tail to the body of the plane
6. Tail fin
7. Support for attaching the wings to the body of the plane
8. Support for attaching the wings to the body of the plane
9. Tail fin

The larger of the small circles are guides for where the rivets should go. The smaller circles are guides for where the nails should go.

Photocopy the triangles below at 200% or print them out from www.phaidon.com/NMT and paste one onto your notepad.

If you want your magic mirror to look like a kaleidoscope, color the triangles in, and stick them in your notepad. You can flick from one pattern to the other, and see the effect in the mirror.

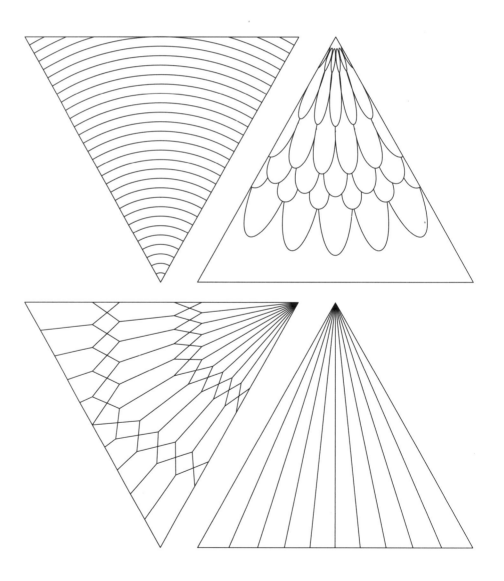

Here are 10 copter templates to choose from! Photocopy them at 100% or print them out from www.phaidon.com/NMT, and then cut them out following the instructions on page 79.

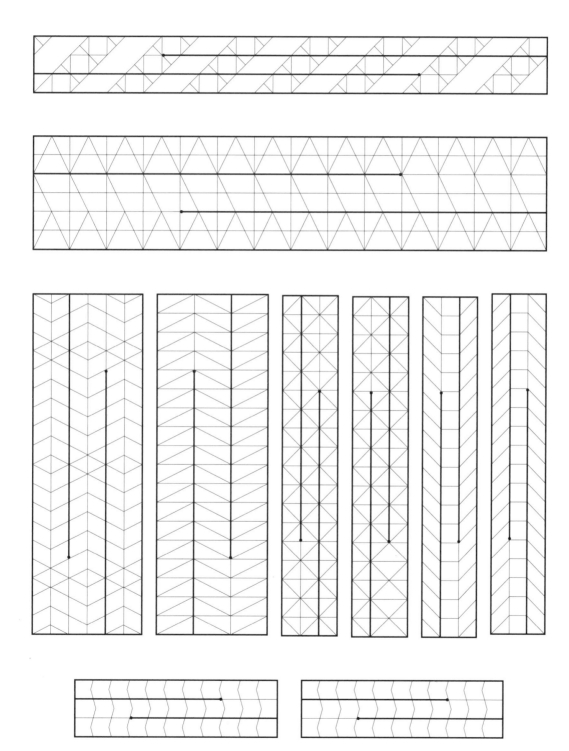

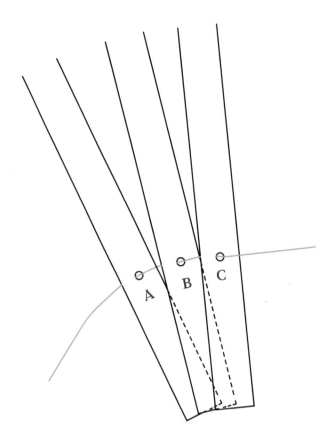

This template for the Candy Lamp needs to be enlarged by six times (600%) and printed out on size E paper (34 x 44 in) at a copy shop, or you can follow the measurements and draw it yourself with a pencil and ruler on a piece of size E paper.

When threading the wool from left to right through the holes in the strips, start at A, as shown above.

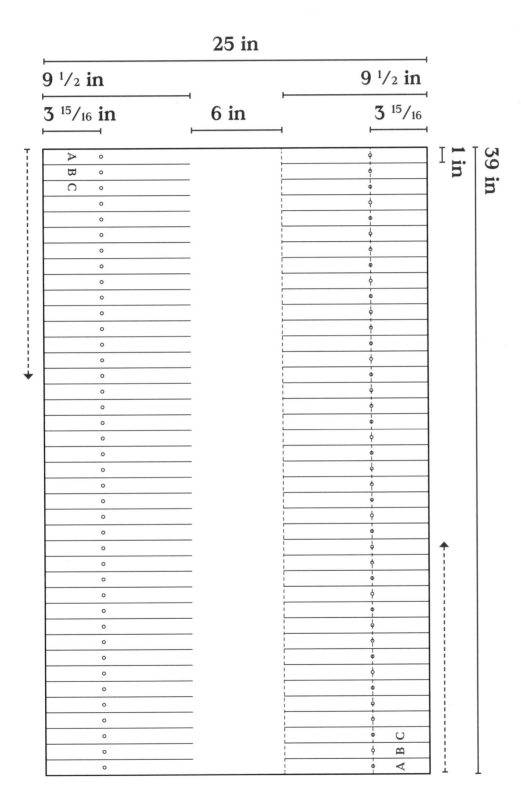

25 in

9 ¹/₂ in

9 ¹/₂ in

3 ¹⁵/₁₆ in

6 in

3 ¹⁵/₁₆

39 in

1 in

A
B
C

A B C

This is a template for the smaller, unlit Candy Ornament. It follows the same steps as the lamp, but you only need 1 $\frac{1}{2}$ feet of yarn and you don't need the light fitting and cable. Go to www.phaidon.com/NMT to print this template out. Follow instruction numbers 1–5 on page 95. Repeat steps 4 and 5 along the strips on the other half of the ornament. Close up the open side of the ornament with a piece of sticky tape.

A B C

A B C

1 Ears
2 Face
3 Tongue

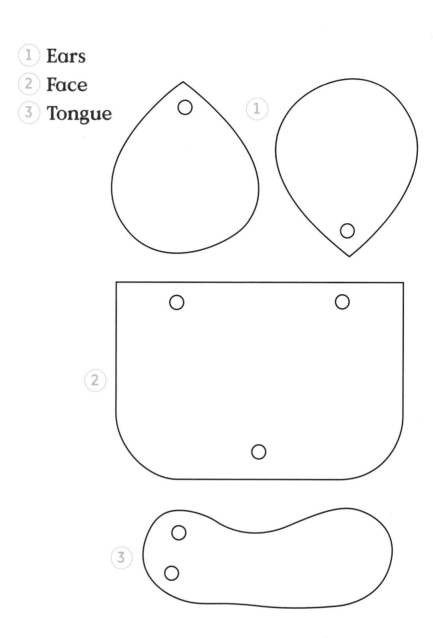

Photocopy this page at 200% or print out the templates from www.phaidon.com/NMT. This pattern will fit a size 4 shoe. Depending on your shoe size, you may need to make the shapes slightly smaller or larger. Make a test-critter from paper first, to check whether the shapes fit your shoes, then copy all the shapes onto a piece of leather (or different pieces, if you want your critters to be multicolored) and cut them out.

① Latch

② D disks (x 3)

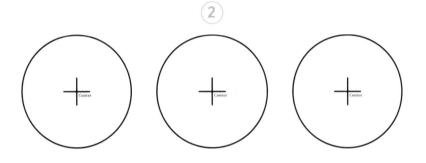

Print out the the templates for your latch and three discs from www.phaidon.com/NMT. Transfer them onto a wooden slat. Ask a grown-up to help you saw out the shapes with a coping saw. To saw out the hole in your latch, ask a grown-up to drill a small hole in the circle marked "A". Release the blade from the saw, pass it through the hole, and then reattach it. Ask an adult to help saw out the circle, following the lines of your template. Smooth down all your sawn edges with sandpaper.

ACKNOWLEDGMENTS

We would like to thank all the designers and their colleagues who developed the projects for this book. The idea for the book was inspired by a series of articles published in the *Süddeutsche Zeitung* magazine, which featured DIY projects by various designers.

NOTE ON SAFETY

This book and the projects presented in this book are designed for children but assume adult supervision at all times. Children's abilities vary by age and by child, and although we take care to identify any hazards, we do not take any responsibility for your children during the preparation and making of these projects. It is up to parents and caregivers to choose age-appropriate projects and materials and to ensure the safety of the children under their supervision.

PHOTOGRAPHY

P.8: Private / P.9: Jonathan Mauloubier, Styling: Silke Schmelzer / P.12: Gerhardt Kellerman / P.13: Jonathan Mauloubier / P.16: Private / P.17: Jonathan Mauloubier, Styling: Silke Schmelzer / P.20: Julien Carreyn / P.21: Jonathan Mauloubier / P.22: istock/ P.24: Private / P.25: Jonathan Mauloubier, Styling: Silke Schmelzer / P.26: istock / P.28: Koos Breukel / P.29: Jonathan Mauloubier / P.32: Inga Knölke / P.33: Jonathan Mauloubier / P.34: istock/ P.36: Private / P.37: Ladies & Gentlemen Studio / P.40: Private / P.41: Jonathan Mauloubier / P.44: Jiaxi Yang & Zhu Zhe / P.45: Jonathan Mauloubier / P.48: Private / P.49: Jonathan Mauloubier / P.52: Private / P.53: Jonathan Mauloubier / P.53: istock/ P.56: Private / P.57: Kobi Benezri/ P.58: istock/ P.60: Toni Meneguzzo / P.61: Jonathan Mauloubier / P.64: Angus Mill / P.65: Jonathan Mauloubier / P.66: istock / P.68: Morten Jerichau / P.69: Jonathan Mauloubier / P.70: istock/ P.72: Private / P.73: Myungsik Jang / P.76: Hadley Hudson / P.77: Jonathan Mauloubier / P.80: Rainer Hosch / P.81: Photo: Jonathan Mauloubier, Styling: Silke Schmelzer / P.84: Tom Nagy / P.85: Jonathan Mauloubier / P.88: Private / P.89: Photo: Jonathan Mauloubier, Styling: Silke Schmelzer / P.92: Gregory Brandel / P.93: Elise Fouin / P.94: istock / P.96: Private / P.97: Elia Mangia / P.100: Knut Koivisto 2010 / P. 101: Jonathan Mauloubier / P:102: istock

All illustrations were designed and executed for this book by Claudia Klein, based on the instructions provided by each designer.

Translation by Ruth Ahmedzai Kemp and Jessica West.

Phaidon Press Inc.
65 Bleecker Street
New York, NY 10012

phaidon.com

First published 2018
© 2018 Phaidon Press Limited
ISBN 978 0 7148 7530 9 (US edition)
004-0218

A CIP catalogue record for this book is available from Library of Congress.

All rights reserved. No part of this publication may be reproduced, stored, in a retrieval system or transmitted, in any form or by any means, electronic, mechanical, photocopying, recording or otherwise, without any written permission of Phaidon Press Limited.

Commissioning editor: Cecily Kaiser
Project editor: Maya Gartner
Production controller: Rebecca Price

Designers: Meagan Bennett, Anna Sullivan
Picture editor: Martina Borsche
Illustrator: Claudia Klein